GIFTS GALORE
in Plastic Canvas

When you give a handmade gift, you share the greatest gift of all – a piece of your heart. This treasury of plastic canvas designs offers ideas for every occasion, from birthdays and weddings to visits from the Tooth Fairy. For whatever reason you need a gift, you'll discover the perfect present here!

LEISURE ARTS, INC.
MAUMELLE, ARKANSAS

TABLE OF CONTENTS

BABY'S HERE!

Help the proud parents announce baby's arrival with this charming door decoration! It's perfect for the nursery, the front door, or even Mom's hospital room. For a baby girl, simply change the message, stitch the border in pink, and give the teddy a pretty pink bow.

NEW BABY DOOR DECORATION

Skill Level: Intermediate

Size: 17³/₄"w x 12¹/₂"h

Supplies: Worsted weight yarn (refer to color key), one 13⁵/₈" x 21⁵/₈" sheet of 5 mesh plastic canvas, #16 tapestry needle, sawtooth hanger, 8" length of ³/₈"w satin ribbon, and clear-drying craft glue or hot glue gun and glue sticks

Stitches Used: Backstitch, Overcast Stitch, and Tent Stitch

Instructions: Use two strands of yarn for all stitches, unless otherwise indicated in color key. (**Note:** Checkerboard and words may be stitched in pink or blue.) Follow chart and use required stitches to work New Baby Door Decoration. Complete background with white Tent Stitches, leaving shaded area unworked. Follow Boy Chart or Girl Chart to work shaded area, completing background with white Tent Stitches. Tie ribbon in a bow and trim ends. Refer to photo to glue bow to bear. For hanger, glue sawtooth hanger to wrong side of stitched piece.

New Baby Door Decoration designed by Maryanne Moreck.

COLOR KEY

⬜	black - 2 yds	⬜	lt blue - 28 yds
⬜	black - 1 strand	⬜	lt brown - 11 yds
⬜	lt pink - 15 yds	⬜	white - 88 yds
⬛	dk brown - 4 yds	⬜	brown - 22 yds
⬜	gold - 7 yds	⬜	pink - 15 yds
⬜	green - 22 yds	⬜	lt gold - 13 yds
⬜	blue - 27 yds		

Boy Chart

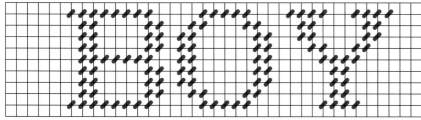

Girl Chart

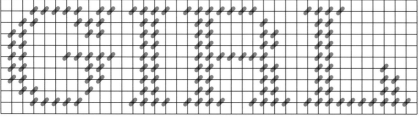

Door Decoration (89 x 63 threads)

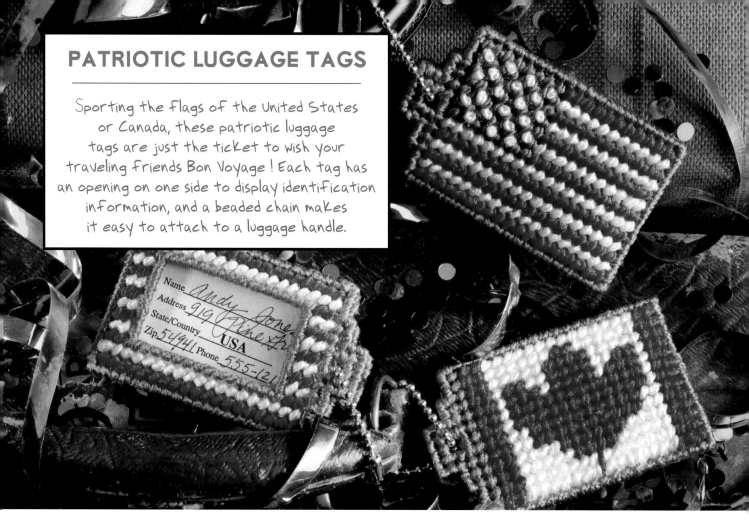

PATRIOTIC LUGGAGE TAGS

Sporting the flags of the United States or Canada, these patriotic luggage tags are just the ticket to wish your traveling friends Bon Voyage! Each tag has an opening on one side to display identification information, and a beaded chain makes it easy to attach to a luggage handle.

LUGGAGE TAGS

Skill Level: Beginner
Size: 3⅝"w x 2¼"h
Supplies: Worsted weight yarn or Needloft® Plastic Canvas Yarn (refer to color key), one 10½" x 13½" sheet of 7 mesh plastic canvas, #16 tapestry needle, and bead chain key ring
Stitches Used: Backstitch, French Knot, Overcast Stitch, and Tent Stitch
Instructions: Follow charts and use required stitches to work Luggage Tag pieces. Use gold to join Front to Back along unworked edges. Refer to photo to attach bead chain key ring to Luggage Tag.

Luggage Tags designed by Diane Villano.

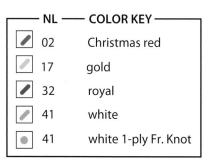

NL	COLOR KEY
02	Christmas red
17	gold
32	royal
41	white
41	white 1-ply Fr. Knot

United States Front (24 x 15 threads)

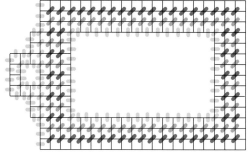

United States Back (24 x 15 threads)

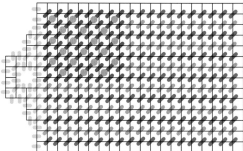

Canada Front (24 x 15 threads)

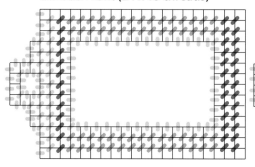

Canada Back (24 x 15 threads)

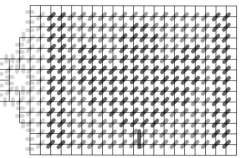

CHARMING BIRDHOUSE

For a gift that's sure to please a bird-watching friend, this ingenious decorative birdhouse is top-flight! A charming way to bring a bit of nature indoors, it's trimmed with pretty flowers and a tiny bird.

BIRDHOUSE

Skill Level: Beginner
Size: 8¹/₂"w x 7"h x 8"d
Supplies: Worsted weight yarn (refer to color key), three 10¹/₂" x 13¹/₂" sheets of 7 mesh plastic canvas, #16 tapestry needle, 36" of ¹/₄"w braided jute ribbon, five 14" lengths of satin ribbon (refer to photo), silk flowers, lightweight artificial bird, 2¹/₂" long twig or dowel for perch, and clear-drying craft glue or hot glue gun and glue sticks
Stitches Used: Backstitch, Gobelin Stitch, Overcast Stitch, Scotch Stitch, and Tent Stitch

Instructions: Follow charts and use required stitches to work Birdhouse pieces. For Back, work Front, completing Scotch Stitch pattern and omitting brown stitches in center. Use lt brown to join Sides along long unworked edges. Use lt brown to join Front and Back to Sides. Use brown to join Roof pieces along unworked edges. Refer to photo and use brown to tack Roof to Front, Back, and Sides. Glue perch to Front. Glue bird to perch. Glue jute ribbon to Roof. Glue flowers to Birdhouse. Tie ribbon lengths together in a bow. Glue bow to flowers.

Birdhouse designed by Dolores Faihst.

	COLOR KEY
	brown - 98 yds
	brown - 2 strands
	lt brown - 87 yds

Roof (54 x 40 threads) (Work 2)

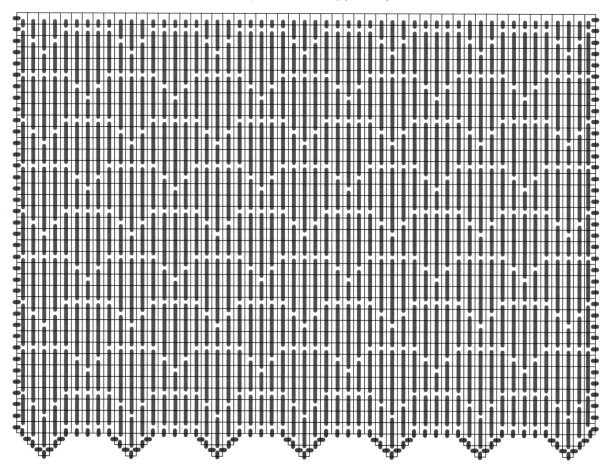

Side (38 x 32 threads) (Work 2)

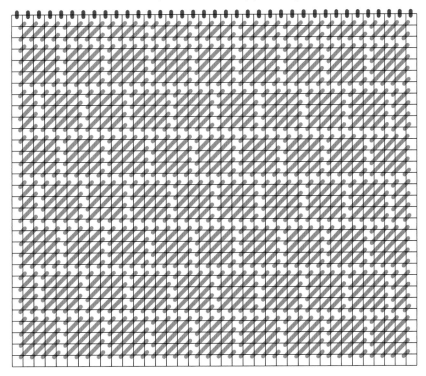

Front/Back (44 x 44 threads) (Cut 2, Work 1)

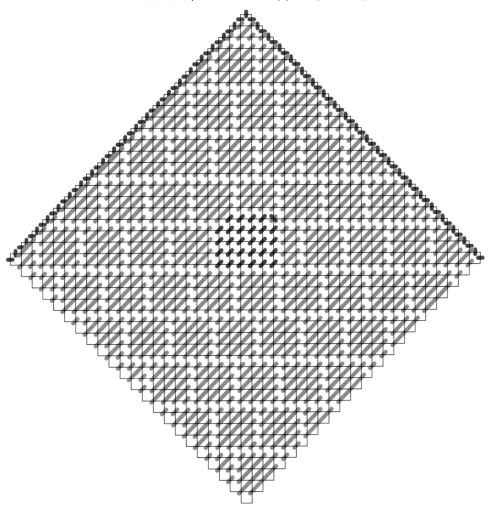

TOOTH FAIRY

Skill Level: Intermediate

Size: 8"w x 10½"h

Supplies: Worsted weight yarn (refer to color key), metallic silver yarn, two 10½" x 13½" sheets of 7 mesh plastic canvas, #16 tapestry needle, curly blonde doll hair, 96" of 7"w white tulle, VELCRO® brand fastening tape, sewing needle, white thread, clear-drying craft glue

Stitches Used: Alternating Scotch Stitch, Backstitch, Cross Stitch, Gobelin Stitch, Overcast Stitch, and Tent Stitch

Instructions: Follow charts and use required stitches to work Tooth Fairy pieces. For hanger, thread 24" of pink yarn through Body Back at ✱'s. Tie yarn in a knot on wrong side of Body Back. Use yarn to match stitching area for all joining. With right sides together, match ▲'s to join Wing A to Body Back.

With right sides together, match ◆'s to join Wing B to Body Back. Join Lower Leg Fronts to Lower Leg Backs, leaving area between ♦'s open. Join Upper Legs together along side edges. Match ♦'s to join Upper Legs to Lower Legs. Join Arm A pieces to Arm B pieces, leaving area between ♠'s open. With wrong sides together, place Body Front on Body Back. Refer to photo and match ♠'s to join Arms to Body Front and Body Back. Match ✦'s to join Upper Legs to Body Front and Body Back. Join Body Front to Body Back along remaining unworked edges. Refer to photo and follow manufacturer's instructions to glue hair to Body Front and Body Back. Cut a 9" length of dk pink yarn. Tie yarn in a bow and trim ends. Glue bow to hair. Cut four 9" lengths of metallic silver yarn. Tie three lengths of metallic yarn

into bows and trim ends. Glue bows to Body Front and Lower Leg Fronts. For tutu, fold tulle in half lengthwise. Use sewing needle and a double thickness of thread to baste long edges together ¼" from edges. Gather tulle to measure 5". Place tutu around Body; tie ends of basting threads together to secure. For Pouch, join Pouch Front to Pouch Side. Join Pouch Side to Pouch Back along unworked edges. Glue Tooth to Pouch Front. For closure, sew VELCRO® fastening tape to Pouch Front and wrong side of Pouch Back. Place remaining metallic yarn length around neck and under Arm. Glue metallic yarn ends to Pouch Side.

Tooth Fairy designed by Jack Peatman for LuvLee Designs.

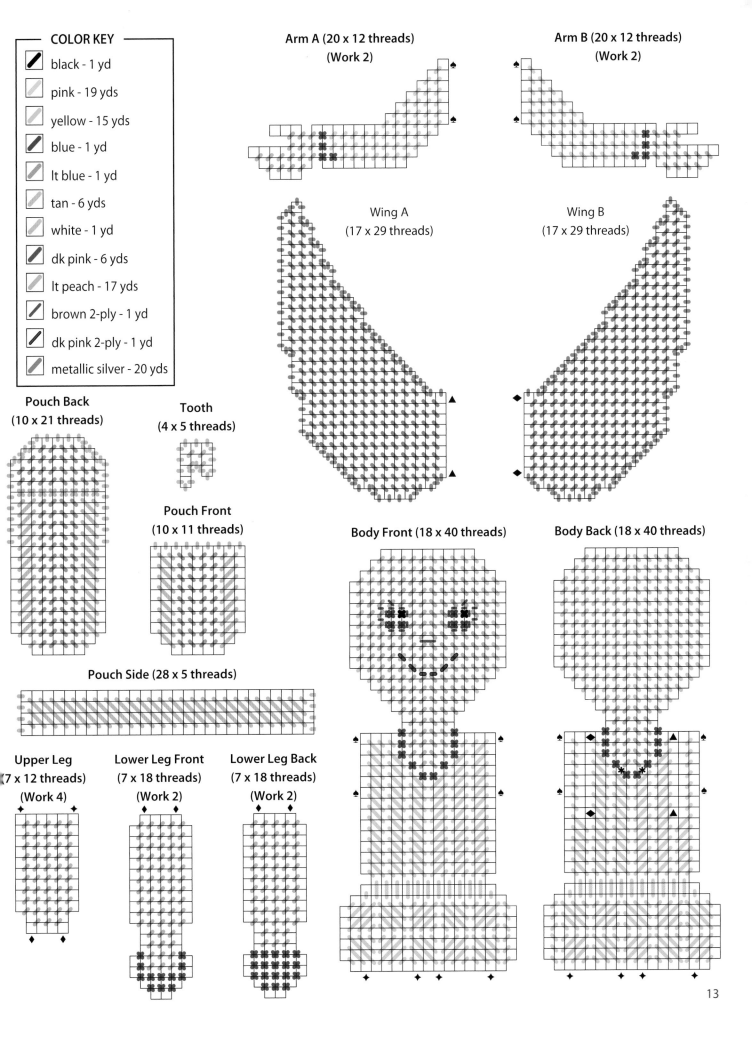

COLOR KEY

- black - 1 yd
- pink - 19 yds
- yellow - 15 yds
- blue - 1 yd
- lt blue - 1 yd
- tan - 6 yds
- white - 1 yd
- dk pink - 6 yds
- lt peach - 17 yds
- brown 2-ply - 1 yd
- dk pink 2-ply - 1 yd
- metallic silver - 20 yds

Arm A (20 x 12 threads)
(Work 2)

Arm B (20 x 12 threads)
(Work 2)

Wing A
(17 x 29 threads)

Wing B
(17 x 29 threads)

Pouch Back
(10 x 21 threads)

Tooth
(4 x 5 threads)

Pouch Front
(10 x 11 threads)

Body Front (18 x 40 threads)

Body Back (18 x 40 threads)

Pouch Side (28 x 5 threads)

Upper Leg
(7 x 12 threads)
(Work 4)

Lower Leg Front
(7 x 18 threads)
(Work 2)

Lower Leg Back
(7 x 18 threads)
(Work 2)

LADYBUG, LADYBUG

For a nice gift in a hurry, dress up a purchased plant with our whimsical ladybug plant poke. The fast-to-finish project adds a personal touch to your presentation, and it's easy enough for beginning stitchers, too.

LADYBUG PLANT POKE
Skill Level: Beginner
Size: 3"w x 4³/₄"h
Supplies: Worsted weight yarn (refer to color key), one 10¹/₂" x 13¹/₂" sheet of 7 mesh plastic canvas, #16 tapestry needle, wooden skewer, 3" length of 3mm black chenille stem, and clear-drying craft glue
Stitches Used: Backstitch, Overcast Stitch, and Tent Stitch
Instructions: Follow chart and use required stitches to work Ladybug. Fold chenille stem in half. Refer to photo to bend and glue chenille stem to wrong side of Ladybug. Glue one end of wooden skewer to wrong side of Ladybug.

Ladybug Plant Poke designed by Dick Martin.

COLOR KEY

✎	black - 2 yds
✎	red - 4 yds

Ladybug (20 x 20 threads)

A TO Z BOOKENDS

Encourage a youngster's love for reading with a set of these brightly colored bookend covers! Presented with several children's books, the clever projects are sure to stimulate a child's interest in learning about everything from apples to zebras!

A TO Z BOOKENDS

Skill Level: Intermediate

Size: 5"w x 5½"h x 2"d

(**Note:** Fit 4¾"w x 5"h bookends.)

Supplies: Worsted weight yarn (refer to color key), two 10½" x 13½" sheets of 7 mesh clear plastic canvas, #16 tapestry needle, two purchased bookends, and clear-drying craft glue

Stitches Used: Backstitch, French Knot, Gobelin Stitch, Overcast Stitch, and Tent Stitch

Instructions: Follow charts and use required stitches to work Bookend pieces, leaving stitches in pink shaded area unworked. Use green and match ★'s to join A Bookend Front to A Base. Refer to photo and use red to tack Apple to A Bookend Front and A Base. Use yarn color to match stitching area to join Back to wrong side of A Bookend Front. Use green and match ✖'s to join Z Bookend Front to Z Base. With right sides facing up, match ▲'s and work stitches in shaded area through two thicknesses to join Zebra to Zebra Support. Use blue and match ■'s to tack Zebra Support to Z Bookend Front. Use black to tack Zebra to Z Base. Use color to match stitching area to join Back to wrong side of Z Bookend Front. For tail, cut three 12" lengths and two 8" lengths of black yarn. Fold three 12" yarn lengths in half and secure fold with one 8" yarn length. Braid for 2" and secure end of braid with remaining yarn length. Trim ends to ½". Remove yarn securing fold. Glue folded end of tail to wrong side of Zebra.

Bookend Covers designed by Dick Martin.

COLOR KEY

✎	black - 5 yds	◢	white - 4 yds
◢	red - 4 yds	◢	yellow - 9 yds
◢	green - 12 yds	●	black Fr. Knot
◢	blue - 20 yds	◉	yellow Fr. Knot

A Bookend Front/Back (34 x 37 threads) (Cut 2, Work 1)

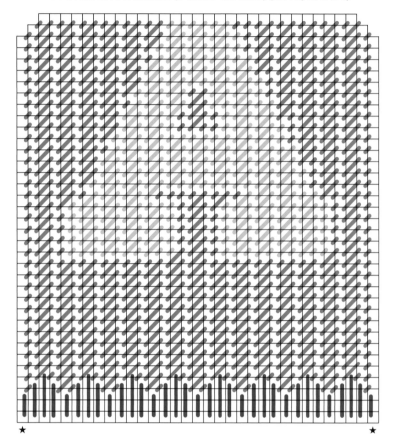

Apple (28 x 24 threads)

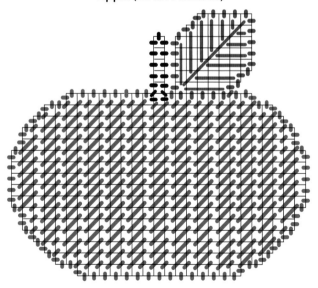

A Base (34 x 14 threads)

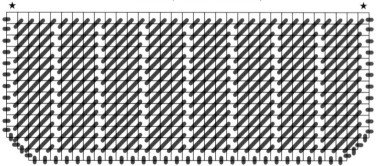

Z Bookend Front/Back (34 x 37 threads) (Cut 2, Work 1)

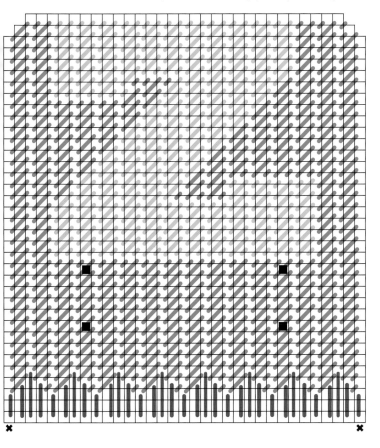

Zebra (27 x 25 threads)

Z Base (34 x 14 threads)

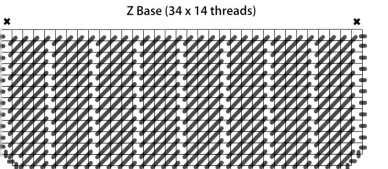

Zebra Support (24 x 7 threads)

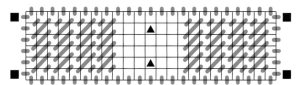

FLOWER GARDEN MAGNETS

Capture the beauty of a flower garden with these lovely magnets. The dainty stick-ups make sweet "thinking of you" gifts for any reason — or no reason at all. Why not make lots of them for sharing a breath of spring all through the year!

FLORAL MAGNETS

Skill Level: Intermediate

Approx Size: 3 1/2"w x 3"h x 1/2"d

Supplies: Worsted weight yarn (refer to color key), one 10 1/2" x 13 1/2" sheet of 7 mesh plastic canvas, #16 tapestry needle, 8" lengths of 1/16"w or 1/4"w satin ribbon (refer to photo), magnetic strip, and clear-drying craft glue

Stitches Used: Backstitch, Cross Stitch, French Knot, Gobelin Stitch, Overcast Stitch, and Tent Stitch

Instructions: Follow charts and use required stitches to work desired Magnet pieces, leaving stitches in blue shaded area unworked. Refer to photo to glue Flowers and Leaves to Wreath, Vase, Basket, and Bouquet. Tie ribbons in a bow and trim ends. Glue bow to stitched piece. Trim magnetic strip to desired size and glue to wrong side of stitched piece.

For Pot only: Refer to photo to stack Petals on Pot Back. Work stitches in shaded area through three thicknesses to join Petals to Pot Back. Place Pot Back on unworked Pot Back. Use yarn color to match stitching area to join Pot Back pieces above ▲'s and between ★'s. With right sides facing up, use blue to join Pot Front to Pot Back pieces.

Basket and Pot designed by Dick Martin.
Wreath designed by Eileen Dobbratz.

COLOR KEY

⊘	lt pink
⊘	brown
⊘	lt green
⊘	blue
⊘	white
⊘	green
⊘	yellow
⊘	Flower #1 desired color
⊘	Flower #2 desired color
◎	lt pink Fr. Knot
○	lt yellow Fr. Knot

Flower #1 (4 x 4 threads)

Flower #2 (6 x 6 threads)

Vase (11 x 20 threads)

Pot Front (19 x 18 threads)

Leaves (10 x 6 threads)

Bouquet (13 x 18 threads)

Wreath (16 x 16 threads)

Pot Back (25 x 25 threads) (Cut 2, Work 1)

Petals (12 x 12 threads) (Work 2)

Basket (24 x 24 threads)

19

BE-HAPPY BEE

A cheery pick-me-up for a friend who's feeling down, this bright-eyed bee is all abuzz about spreading sunshine. The cute stick-up is easily attached with suction cups to windows or any glass surface. Wearing a broad smile and a snazzy bow tie, our little friend shares the sentiment, "Don't worry, 'Bee' Happy!"

BEE HAPPY STICK-UP

Skill Level: Intermediate

Size: 5⅝"w x 6½"h

Supplies: Worsted weight yarn (refer to color key), one 10½" x 13½" sheet of 7 mesh plastic canvas, #16 tapestry needle, 8" length of 3mm black chenille stem, two 20mm suction cups, two 15mm moving eyes, and clear-drying craft glue

Stitches Used: Backstitch, French Knot, Gobelin Stitch, Overcast Stitch, Tent Stitch, and Triple Cross Stitch

Instructions: Follow charts and use required stitches to work Stick-up pieces. Insert and glue suction cups into openings in Front at ▲'s. Cut chenille stem in half. Refer to photo to bend and glue chenille stem pieces to wrong side of Front. With wrong sides together, use color to match stitching area to join Front to Back along unworked edges. Refer to photo to glue Nose, Bow Tie, and moving eyes to Front. For mouth, cut a 3" length of black yarn. Refer to photo to shape and glue black yarn to Front.

Bee Happy Stick-up designed by Sandy and Honey for Studio M.

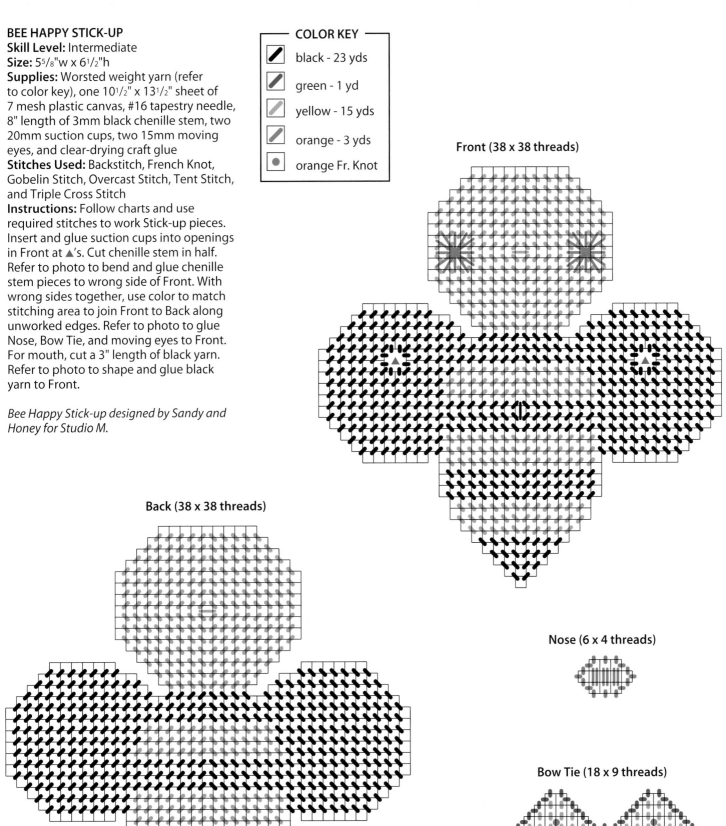

COLOR KEY

- ✎ black - 23 yds
- ✎ green - 1 yd
- ✎ yellow - 15 yds
- ✎ orange - 3 yds
- ● orange Fr. Knot

Front (38 x 38 threads)

Back (38 x 38 threads)

Nose (6 x 4 threads)

Bow Tie (18 x 9 threads)

"BEARY" SPECIAL RELATIVES

Show family members that they're appreciated with these adorable personalized magnets! Perfect as thank-you gifts, forget-me-nots, or for any family occasion, they're "beary" special reminders of your love. The miniature flocked bears can be positioned anywhere along the rainbow to punctuate your sweet sentiments.

SPECIAL RELATIVES MAGNET

Skill Level: Beginner

Size: 4¹⁄₈"w x 2⁵⁄₈"h x ³⁄₄"d

Supplies: Worsted weight yarn (refer to color key), six-strand black embroidery floss, one 10¹⁄₂" x 13¹⁄₂" sheet of 7 mesh plastic canvas, #16 tapestry needle, 1" flocked bear, magnetic strip, and clear-drying craft glue

Stitches Used: Backstitch, Overcast Stitch, and Tent Stitch

Instructions: Follow chart and use required stitches to work Magnet. Refer to photo to center and stitch desired name. Glue flocked bear to stitched piece. Trim magnetic strip to desired size and glue to wrong side of stitched piece.

Special Relatives Magnets designed by Toni Erwin.

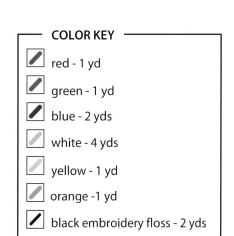

COLOR KEY

▨	red - 1 yd
▨	green - 1 yd
▨	blue - 2 yds
▨	white - 4 yds
▨	yellow - 1 yd
▨	orange -1 yd
▨	black embroidery floss - 2 yds

Magnet (28 x 18 threads)

FOR YOUR FAVORITE FOLKS

These fun magnets are great for saying "you're special" to a friend or family member. The cute messages will put a smile on anyone's face!

MAGNETS

Skill Level: Beginner

Approx Size: 4"w x 4"h each

Supplies: Worsted weight yarn (refer to color key), 6-strand embroidery floss (refer to color key), one 10½" x 13½" sheet of 7 mesh plastic canvas, #16 tapestry needle, magnetic strip, and clear-drying craft glue

Stitches Used: Backstitch, Overcast Stitch, and Tent Stitch

Instructions: Follow chart and use required stitches to work Magnet. Trim magnetic strip to desired size and glue to wrong side of stitched piece.

Magnets designed by Kathleen Hurley.

COLOR KEY

✎	red - 6 yds
✎	brown - 2 yds
✎	green - 1 yd
✎	dk green - 1 yd
✎	ecru - 6 yds
✎	tan - 2 yds
✎	blue embroidery floss - 2 yds
✎	black embroidery floss - 2 yds

Apple (21 x 26 threads)

Cup (34 x 22 threads)

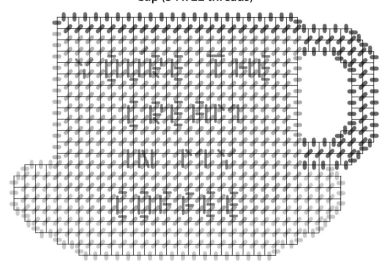

BIRTHDAY BALLOONS

Brighten a friend's birthday outlook with brilliant balloons! This "uplifting" eyeglasses case is a fun way to protect lenses from scratches. Quick and easy enough for a beginner, it's also a great way to use up scrap yarn!

BALLOON EYEGLASSES CASE
Skill Level: Beginner
Size: 3³/₄"w x 6³/₄"h
Supplies: Worsted weight yarn (refer to color key), one 10¹/₂" x 13¹/₂" sheet of 7 mesh plastic canvas, and #16 tapestry needle

Stitches Used: Backstitch, Overcast Stitch, and Tent Stitch
Instructions: Follow chart and use required stitches to work Balloon Eyeglasses Case pieces. With wrong sides together, use black to join Front to Back along unworked edges.

Balloon Eyeglasses Case designed by Kathy Sarnelli.

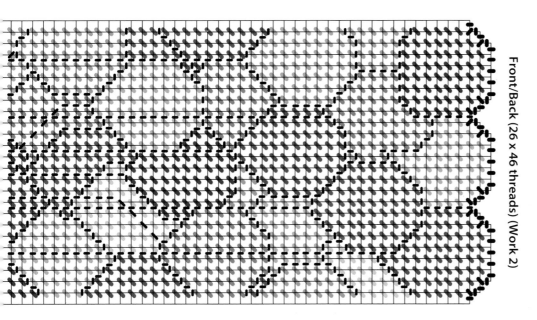

Front/Back (26 x 46 threads) (Work 2)

COLOR KEY

black - 15 yds	aqua - 3 yds
red - 7 yds	melon - 4 yds
green - 5 yds	yellow - 6 yds
blue - 5 yds	purple - 6 yds
pink - 3 yds	

A CUP OF FRIENDSHIP

This charming teacup magnet is a sweet token of friendship, and it's so easy you can probably finish it before the kettle whistles! The double-sided magnet is left open at the top to form a pocket for holding a tea bag. A heart-shaped gift tag, tied onto the bag's string, can be penned with poetry, an encouraging thought, or any sentiment appropriate for the occasion.

A LITTLE CUP OF FRIENDSHIP, WITH A BAG OF TEA. WHEN YOU DRINK THIS THINK OF LOVE FROM ME!

CUP OF TEA MAGNET
Skill Level: Beginner
Size: 3½"w x 2¾"h
Supplies: worsted weight yarn or Needloft® Plastic Canvas Yarn (refer to color key), one 10½" x 13½" sheet of 7 mesh plastic canvas, #16 tapestry needle, magnetic strip, and clear-drying craft glue

Stitches Used: Overcast Stitch and Tent Stitch
Instructions: Follow charts and use required stitches to work Magnet pieces. With wrong sides together, use eggshell to join Front to Back along unworked edges. Glue magnetic strip to Back.

Cup of Tea Magnet designed by Fran Way Bohler.

NL COLOR KEY

	NL	
✎		desired color - 3 yds
✎	39	eggshell - 9 yds

Front (24 x 18 threads)

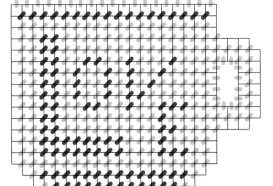

Back (24 x 18 threads)

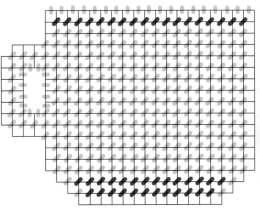

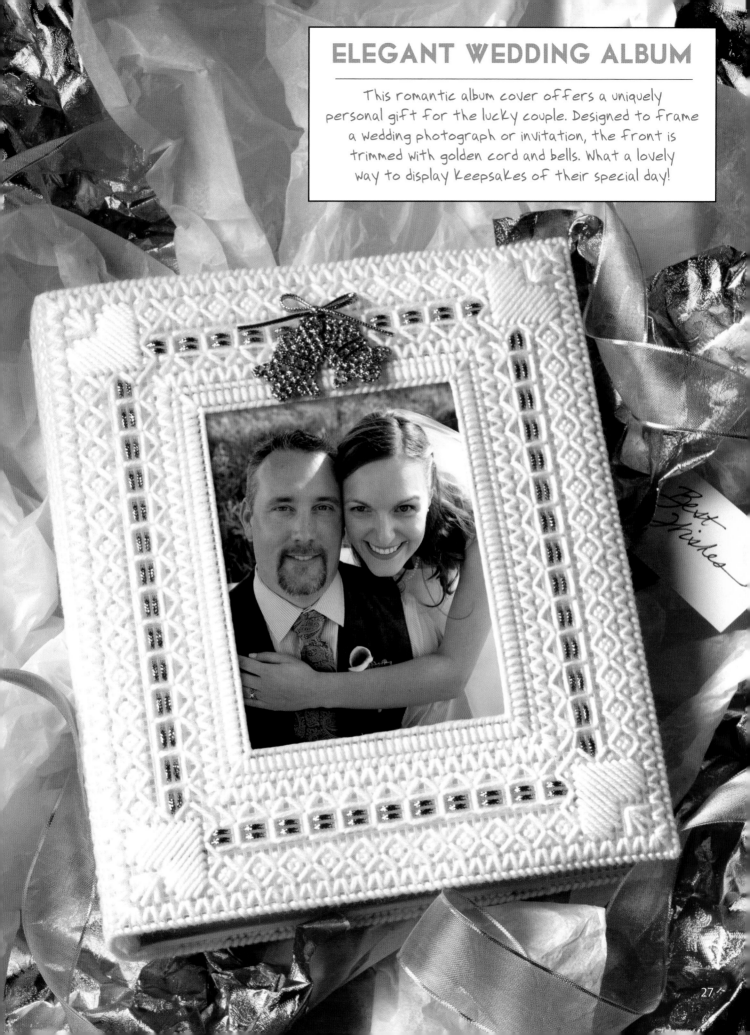

ELEGANT WEDDING ALBUM

This romantic album cover offers a uniquely personal gift for the lucky couple. Designed to frame a wedding photograph or invitation, the front is trimmed with golden cord and bells. What a lovely way to display keepsakes of their special day!

WEDDING ALBUM COVER

Skill Level: Intermediate

Size: 10¼"w x 12"h x 2⅝"d
(**Note:** Fits a 9½"w x 11½"h x 2½"d photo album and holds a 5"w x 7"h photograph.)

Supplies: White worsted weight yarn, metallic gold cord, three 10½" x 13½" sheets of 7 mesh plastic canvas, #16 tapestry needle, photo album, and clear-drying craft glue

Stitches Used: Alternating Scotch Stitch, Backstitch, Gobelin Stitch, and Overcast Stitch

Instructions: Follow charts and use required stitches to work Wedding Album Cover pieces, leaving stitches in pink shaded areas unworked. For Back, cut a piece of plastic canvas 68 x 80 threads. Use white Alternating Scotch Stitches over three threads to work Back. For Photo Backing, cut a piece of plastic canvas 38 x 50 threads. Match Photo Backing edges to shaded areas on wrong side of Front. Work stitches in shaded areas to join Photo Backing to Front. Use white for all joining. Refer to photo to join Spine to Front and Back along long edges. For Sleeves, cut two pieces of plastic canvas 15 x 80 threads each. Match corners of Sleeve to ▲'s on wrong side of Front to join Sleeve to Front. Repeat for Back and remaining Sleeve. Use white Overcast Stitches to cover unworked edges of Front, Back, and Spine. For bow, cut an 8" length of metallic gold cord. Tie cord in a bow and trim ends. Refer to photo to glue Bells and bow to Front.

Wedding Album Cover designed by Dick Martin.

COLOR KEY

- white - 187 yds
- metallic gold cord - 19 yds

Bell (11 x 11 threads) (Work 2)

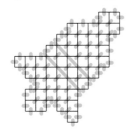

Spine (18 x 80 threads)

CHATELAINE BEAR

This cute chatelaine makes a sweet friendship gift for a "beary" special seamstress. Quick to stitch, the lovable little bear and a pair of scissors are attached to opposite ends of a length of ribbon and worn around the neck. What a clever way to keep a sewing essential handy!

CHATELAINE

Skill Level: Beginner

Bear Size: $2^{5}/_{8}$"w x 4"h

Supplies: Worsted weight yarn (refer to color key), one $10^{1}/_{2}$" x $13^{1}/_{2}$" sheet of 7 mesh plastic canvas, #16 tapestry needle, 48" of $^{3}/_{8}$"w blue grosgrain ribbon, embroidery scissors, sewing needle, and thread

Stitches Used: Backstitch, Cross Stitch, French Knot, Overcast Stitch, and Tent Stitch

Instructions: Follow chart and use required stitches to work Bear. Refer to photo to thread ends of ribbon through Bear and embroidery scissors. Fold ribbon ends under and sew in place.

Chatelaine designed by Kathie Rueger.

COLOR KEY

╱	black 2-ply
╱	red
╱	brown
╱	dk brown
╱	dk brown 2-ply
╱	tan
●	black Fr. Knot

Bear (18 x 27 threads)

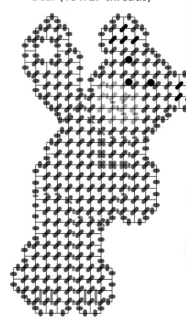

FISHING FOR FUN

This whimsical fishing pond is a fun way to help a preschooler catch on to learning numbers and colors. The rod has a magnet glued to the end of the line that "hooks" paper clips extending from the fishes' mouths. As each fish is caught, the child can identify its color and the number on its side.

FISHING SET

Skill Level: Intermediate

Pond Size: 9¼"w x 9¼"h x 3"d

Supplies: Worsted weight yarn (refer to color key), three 10½" x 13½" sheets of clear 7 mesh plastic canvas, one 10½" x 13½" sheet of dark blue 7 mesh plastic canvas, #16 tapestry needle, two ¾" dia magnets, two 13" lengths of coat hanger wire, ten jumbo wire paper clips, twenty 6mm moving eyes, hot glue gun, and glue sticks

Stitches Used: Backstitch, Cross Stitch, Gobelin Stitch, Overcast Stitch, and Tent Stitch

Instructions: For Pond Bottom, cut a piece of dark blue plastic canvas 65 x 65 threads. (**Note:** Pond Bottom is not worked.) Cut remaining pieces from clear plastic canvas. Refer to photo to work Fish Fronts in colors to match Fish Backs. Follow charts and use required stitches to work remaining Fishing Set pieces. Use color to match stitching area for all joining. Thread wire lengths under Gobelin Stitches on wrong side of Pole Front. With wrong sides together, join Pole Front to Pole Back. Cut a 24" length of yellow yarn. Glue one end of yarn between magnets. Tie remaining yarn end to end of Pole and trim short end close to knot. Join Pond Sides along short edges. Join Pond Sides to Pond Bottom. For each Fish, refer to photo to place one paper clip between wrong sides of Fish Front and Fish Back. Join Fish Front to Fish Back. Refer to photo to glue moving eyes to Fish Front.

Fishing Set designed by Jack Peatman for LuvLee Designs.

COLOR KEY

- black - 17 yds
- red - 9 yds
- green - 9 yds
- royal - 30 yds
- blue - 15 yds
- lt blue - 14 yds
- grey - 10 yds
- white - 16 yds
- yellow - 14 yds
- orange - 9 yds
- bright blue - 9 yds
- bright pink - 9 yds
- purple - 9 yds
- color to match back

Pond Side (65 x 21 threads) (Work 4)

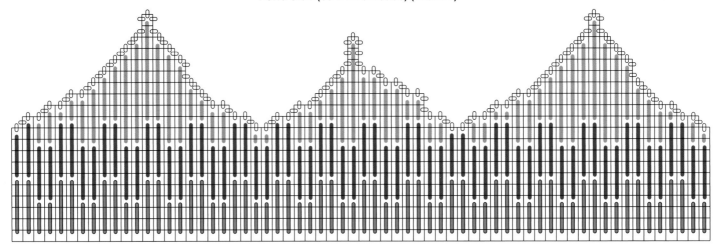

Fish Back (21 x 14 threads each)

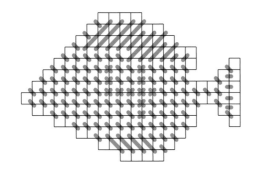
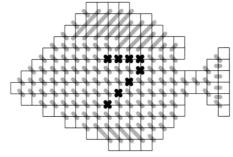
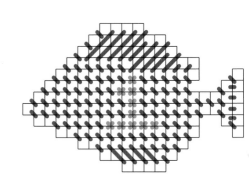

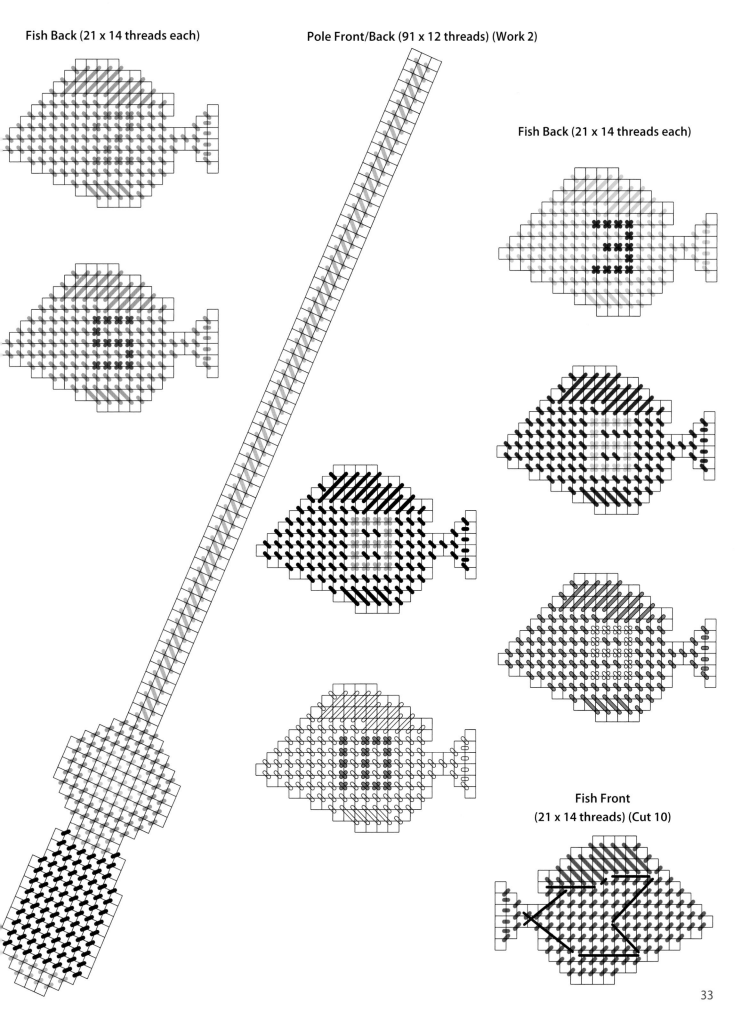

Fish Back (21 x 14 threads each)

Pole Front/Back (91 x 12 threads) (Work 2)

Fish Back (21 x 14 threads each)

**Fish Front
(21 x 14 threads) (Cut 10)**

33

ANNIVERSARY BASKET

Congratulate a special couple on their anniversary with this elegant basket. Stitched with white and gold metallic cord, it's just right for presenting a pair of goblets and a sparkling beverage. Trim the handle with a shiny bow, and your gift will really sparkle!

BASKET

Skill Level: Intermediate
Size: 8"w x 8"h x 5½"d
Supplies: Metallic gold/white cord, two 10½" x 13½" sheets of 7 mesh plastic canvas, and #16 tapestry needle
Stitches Used: Gobelin Stitch, Overcast Stitch, and Tent Stitch
Instructions: Follow chart and use required stitches to work Handle through two thicknesses. Follow charts and use required stitches to work remaining Basket pieces, leaving blue shaded areas unworked. Refer to photo to join Long Sides to Short Sides along short edges. For Bottom, cut a piece of plastic canvas 28 x 52 threads. (**Note:** Bottom is not worked.) Join Sides to Bottom. Match ▲'s and work stitches in shaded areas to join Rim pieces. Match ■'s to tack Handle to right sides of Long Sides. Match unworked edges to place Rim around outside of Sides and Handle. Join Rim to Sides and Handle.

Basket designed by Teal Lee Elliott.

Short Side (28 x 24 threads) (Work 2)

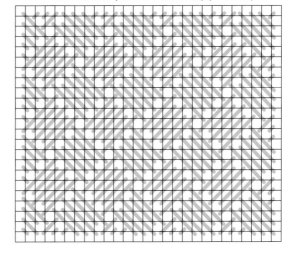

Long Side (52 x 24 threads) (Work 2)

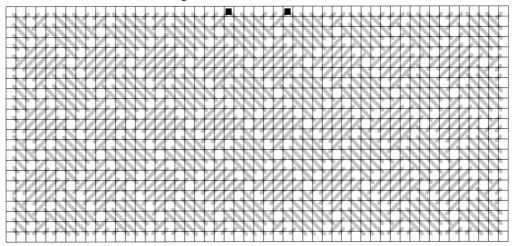

Rim (59 x 7 threads) (Work 3)

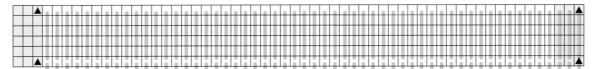

Handle (72 x 8 threads) (Cut 2)

BOOGIE-WOOGIE FRUIT

These colorful dancing fruit magnets will give any friend's memos fresh "a-peel"! Decked out with top hats and canes, they're also cute for displaying children's artwork.

DANCING FRUIT MAGNETS

Skill Level: Beginner

Approx Size: 5"w x 5¹/₂"h

Supplies for each Magnet: Worsted weight yarn (refer to color key), one 10¹/₂" x 13¹/₂" sheet of 7 mesh plastic canvas, #16 tapestry needle, magnetic strip, two 10mm moving eyes, 7mm green pom-pom, 12" length of 3mm black chenille stem, and clear-drying craft glue

Stitches Used: Backstitch, Overcast Stitch, and Tent Stitch

Instructions: Follow charts and use required stitches to work Magnet pieces. Refer to photo to glue eyes and pom-pom to Magnet. For bow, use yarn color to match Feet. Cut an 8" length of yarn. Tie yarn in a bow and trim ends. Glue bow to Magnet. For arms and legs, cut chenille stem in half. Thread chenille stem through canvas. Glue Hands and Feet to ends of chenille stems. Shape arms and legs as desired. Glue Hat and Cane to Magnet. Glue magnetic strip to wrong side of Magnet.

Dancing Fruit Magnets designed by Nova Barta.

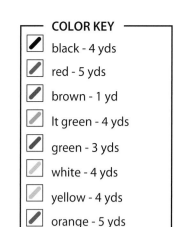

COLOR KEY

✎	black - 4 yds
✎	red - 5 yds
✎	brown - 1 yd
✎	lt green - 4 yds
✎	green - 3 yds
✎	white - 4 yds
✎	yellow - 4 yds
✎	orange - 5 yds
✎	desired color - 4 yds

Banana (11 x 28 threads)

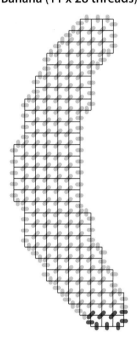

Right Hand (6 x 7 threads)

Left Hand (6 x 7 threads)

Hat (9 x 6 threads)

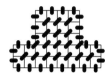

Right Foot (8 x 5 threads)

Left Foot (8 x 5 threads)

Cane (5 x 12 threads)

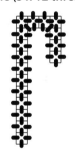

Orange (18 x 22 threads)

Apple (19 x 23 threads)

Pear (16 x 22 threads)

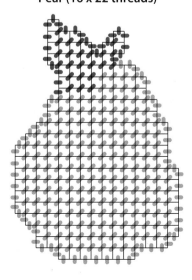

MOTHER'S DAY TISSUE BOX COVER

Surprise your mom on Mother's Day (or any day) with our beautiful floral tissue box cover! Designed to fit a standard-size box of tissues, its soothing colors will add a charming touch of springtime to her decor.

FLORAL TISSUE BOX COVER

Skill Level: Beginner
Size: 10"w x 3¹⁄₂"h x 5¹⁄₄"d
(**Note:** Fits a 9¹⁄₂"w x 3"h x 4³⁄₄"d tissue box.)
Supplies: Worsted weight yarn (refer to color key), two 10¹⁄₂" x 13¹⁄₂" sheets of 7 mesh plastic canvas, and #16 tapestry needle
Stitches Used: Gobelin Stitch, Overcast Stitch, and Tent Stitch
Instructions: Follow charts and use required stitches to work Floral Tissue Box Cover pieces. Use blue for all joining. Join Long Sides to Short Sides along short edges. Join Top to Sides.

COLOR KEY

pink - 14 yds		blue - 46 yds	
lt pink - 9 yds		lt blue - 21 yds	
tan - 15 yds		white - 21 yds	
yellow - 3 yds		green - 9 yds	

Short Side (35 x 23 threads) (Work 2)

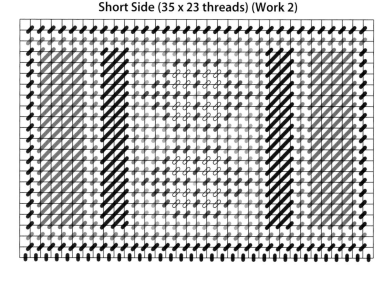

Long Side (67 x 23 threads) (Work 2)

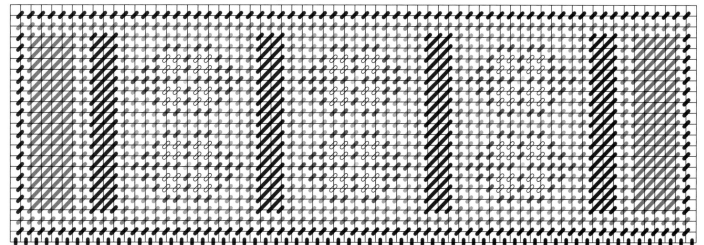

Top (67 x 35 threads)

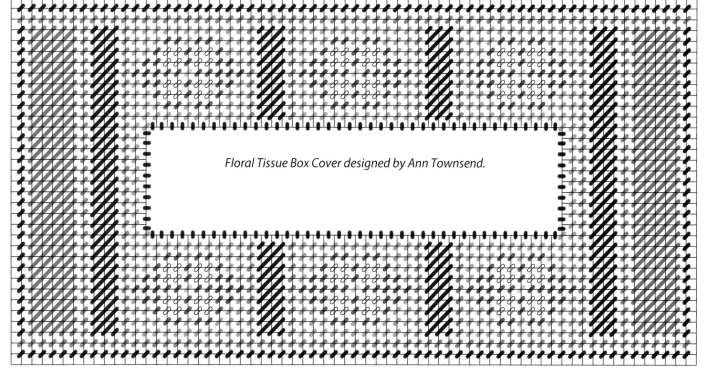

Floral Tissue Box Cover designed by Ann Townsend.

DELIGHTFUL DAISIES

Delight a friend with this daisy boutique tissue box cover.
Its bright colors and cheerful basket design will lend an airy
feel to the bath – or any room – all through the year!

DAISY BASKET TISSUE BOX COVER

Skill Level: Intermediate
Size: 4½"w x 5½"h x 4½"d
(**Note:** Fits a 4¼"w x 5¼"h x 4¼"d boutique tissue box.)
Supplies: Worsted weight yarn (refer to color key), two 10½" x 13½" sheets of 7 mesh plastic canvas, and #16 tapestry needle
Stitches Used: Backstitch, French Knot, Gobelin Stitch, Overcast Stitch, and Tent Stitch
Instructions: Follow charts and use required stitches to work Daisy Basket Tissue Box Cover pieces. Refer to photo for yarn color used for joining. Join Sides along long edges. Join Top to Sides.

Daisy Basket Tissue Box Cover designed by Dick Martin.

COLOR KEY

▧	brown - 27 yds
▧	green - 23 yds
▱	white - 2 strands - 23 yds
▨	yellow - 3 yds
◎	yellow Fr. Knot

Top (42 x 42 threads)

Side (46 x 46 threads)
(Work 4)

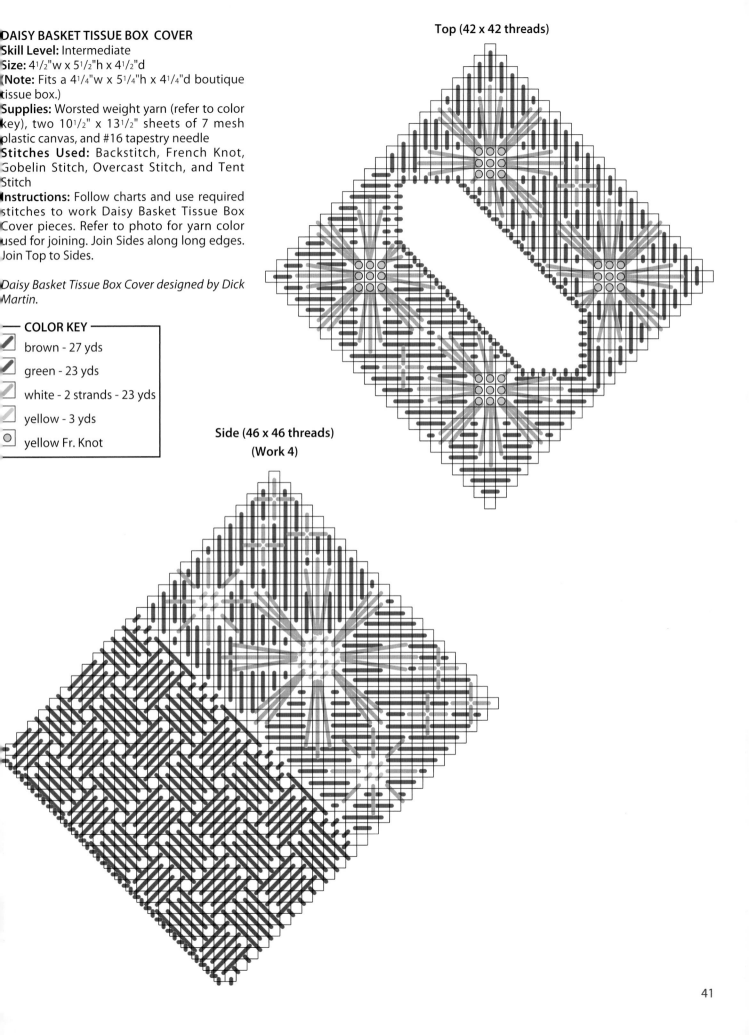

NEIGHBORLY WELCOME

Welcome new neighbors with a houseplant displayed in this cute flowerpot cover! Easy enough for a beginner and inexpensive to make, it's a wonderful way to help friendship bloom.

PLANTER COVER

Skill Level: Beginner
Size: 3"h
Supplies: Sport weight yarn (refer to color key), one 10½" x 13½" sheet of 10 mesh plastic canvas, #20 tapestry needle, and 3"h x 4"dia planter
Stitches Used: Gobelin Stitch, Overcast Stitch, and Tent Stitch
Instructions: For Side, cut a piece of plastic canvas 123 x 29 threads. Follow chart and use required stitches to work Side, repeating charted pattern until piece is completely worked. Use yarn color to match stitching area to join unworked edges, forming a cylinder. Slide Planter Cover over planter.

Planter Cover designed by Ann Townsend.

COLOR KEY
- white
- pink
- dk pink
- blue
- dk blue
- green

Side (123 x 29 threads)

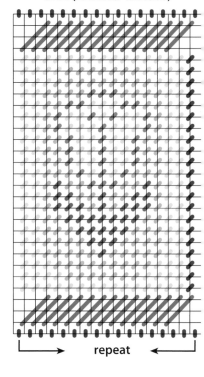

repeat

GENERAL INSTRUCTIONS

SELECTING PLASTIC CANVAS

Plastic canvas is a molded, nonwoven canvas made from clear or colored plastic. The canvas consists of "threads" and "holes." The threads aren't actually "threads" since the canvas is nonwoven, but it seems to be an accurate description of the straight lines of the canvas. The holes, as you would expect, are the spaces between the threads. The threads are often referred to in the project instructions, especially when cutting out plastic canvas pieces. The instructions for stitches will always refer to holes when explaining where to place your needle to make a stitch.

TYPES OF CANVAS

The main difference between types of plastic canvas is the mesh size. Mesh size refers to the number of holes in one inch of canvas. The most common mesh sizes are 5 mesh, 7 mesh, 10 mesh, and 14 mesh. Five mesh means that there are 5 holes in every inch of canvas. Likewise, there are 7 holes in every inch of 7 mesh canvas, 10 holes in every inch of 10 mesh canvas, and 14 holes in every inch of 14 mesh canvas. Seven mesh canvas is the most popular size for the majority of projects.

Your project supply list will tell you what size mesh you need to buy. Be sure to use the mesh size the project instructions recommend. If your project calls for 7 mesh canvas and you use 10 mesh, your finished project will be much smaller than expected. For example, say your instructions tell you to use 7 mesh canvas to make a boutique tissue box cover. You will need to cut each side 30 x 38 threads so they will measure 4½" x 5¾" each. But if you were using 10 mesh canvas your sides would only measure 3" x 3⅞"! Needless to say, your tissue box cover from 10 mesh canvas would not fit a boutique tissue box.

When buying canvas, you may find that some canvas is firm and rigid while other canvas is softer and more pliable. To decide which type of canvas is right for your project, think of how the project will be used. If you are making a box or container, you will want to use firmer canvas so that the box will be sturdy and not buckle after handling. If you are making a tissue box cover, you will not need the firmer canvas because the tissue box will support the canvas and prevent warping. Softer canvas is better for projects that require a piece of canvas to be bent before it is joined to another piece.

AMOUNT OF CANVAS

The project supply list usually tells you how much canvas you will need to complete the project. When buying your canvas, remember that several different manufacturers produce plastic canvas. Therefore, there are often slight variations in canvas, such as different thicknesses of threads or a small difference in mesh size. Because of these variations, try to buy enough canvas for your entire project at the same time and place. As a general rule, it is always better to buy too much canvas and have leftovers than to run out of canvas before you finish your project. By buying a little extra canvas, you not only allow for mistakes, but have extra canvas for practicing your stitches. Scraps of canvas are also excellent for making magnets and other small projects.

SELECTING YARN

Worsted weight yarn is used for most of the projects in this book. Worsted weight yarn has four plies which are twisted together to form one strand. When the instructions indicate 2-ply yarn, separate the strand of yarn and stitch using only two of the four plies.

The color key includes the descriptive color name (**COLOR**) and sometimes the Needloft® Plastic Canvas Yarn numbers (**NL**). Needloft® Yarn is 100% nylon and is suitable only for 7 mesh plastic canvas.

Needloft® Yarn will not easily separate. When the instructions call for "2-ply" or "1-ply" yarn, we recommend that you substitute with six strands of embroidery floss.

TYPES OF YARN

If your finished project will be handled or used a lot, such as a coaster or magnet, you will want to use a durable, washable yarn. We highly recommend acrylic or nylon yarn for plastic canvas. It can be washed repeatedly and holds up well to frequent usage and handling. If your finished project won't be handled or used frequently, such as a framed picture or a bookend, you are not limited to washable yarns.

The types of yarns available are endless and each grouping of yarn has its own characteristics and uses. The following is a brief description of some common yarns used for plastic canvas.

Worsted Weight Yarn - This yarn may be found in acrylic, wool, wool blends, and a variety of other fiber contents. Worsted weight yarn is the most popular yarn used for 7 mesh plastic canvas because one strand covers the canvas very well. This yarn is inexpensive and comes in a wide range of colors. Worsted weight yarn has four plies which are twisted together to form one strand. When the instructions call for "2-ply" or "1-ply" yarn, you will need to separate a strand of yarn into the required number of plies before stitching.

Sport Weight Yarn - This yarn has four thin plies which are twisted together to form one strand. Like worsted weight yarn, sport weight yarn comes in a variety of fiber contents. The color selection in sport weight yarn is more limited than in other types of yarns. You may want to use a double strand of sport weight yarn for better coverage of your 7 mesh canvas. When you plan on doubling your yarn, remember to double the yardage called for in the instructions too. Sport weight yarn works nicely for 10 mesh canvas.

Embroidery Floss - Occasionally embroidery floss is used to add small details such as eyes or mouths on 7 mesh canvas. Twelve strands of embroidery floss are recommended for covering 10 mesh canvas. Use six strands to cover 14 mesh canvas.

COLORS

Choosing colors can be fun, but sometimes a little difficult. Your project will tell you what yarn colors you will need. When you begin searching for the recommended colors, you may be slightly overwhelmed by the different shades of each color. Here are a few guidelines to consider when choosing your colors.

Consider where you are going to place the finished project. If the project is going in a particular room in your house, match your yarn to the room's colors.

Try not to mix very bright colors with dull colors. For example, if you're stitching a project using muted colors, don't use a bright Christmas red with muted blues and greens. Instead, use a maroon or muted red. Likewise, if you are stitching a bright tissue box cover for a child's room, don't use muted blue with bright red, yellow, and green.

Some projects require several shades of a color, such as shades of red for a Santa. Be sure your shades blend well together.

Remember, you don't have to use the colors suggested in the color key. If you find a blue tissue box cover that you really like, but your house is decorated in pink, change the colors in the tissue box cover to pink!

AMOUNTS

A handy way of estimating yardage is to make a yarn yardage estimator. Cut a one yard piece of yarn for each different stitch used in your project. For each stitch, work as many stitches as you can with the one yard length of yarn.

To use your yarn yardage estimator, count the number of stitches you were able to make, say 72 Tent Stitches. Now look at the chart for the project you want to make. Estimate the number of ecru Tent Stitches on the chart, say 150. Now divide the estimated number of ecru stitches by the actual number stitched with a yard of yarn. One hundred fifty divided by 72 is approximately two. So you will need about two yards of ecru yarn to make your project. Repeat this for all stitches and yarn colors. To allow for repairs and practice stitches, purchase extra yardage of each color. If you have yarn left over, remember that scraps of yarn are perfect for small projects such as magnets or when you need just a few inches of a particular color for another project.

In addition to purchasing an adequate amount of each color of yarn, it is also important to buy all of the yarn you need to complete your project at the same time. Yarn often varies in the amount of dye used to color the yarn. Although the variation may be slight when yarns from two different dye lots are held together, the variation is usually very apparent on a stitched piece.

SELECTING NEEDLES
TYPES OF NEEDLES
Stitching on plastic canvas should be done with a blunt needle called a tapestry needle. Tapestry needles are sized by numbers; the higher the number, the smaller the needle. The correct size needle to use depends on the canvas mesh size and the yarn thickness. The needle should be small enough to allow the threaded needle to pass through the canvas holes easily, without disturbing the canvas threads. The eye of the needle should be large enough to allow yarn to be threaded easily. If the eye is too small, yarn will wear thin and may break. You will find the recommended needle size listed in the supply section of each project.

WORKING WITH PLASTIC CANVAS
Throughout this book the lines of the canvas will be referred to as threads. However, they are not actually "threads" since the canvas is nonwoven. To cut plastic canvas pieces accurately, count **threads** (not **holes**) as shown in Fig. 1.

Fig. 1

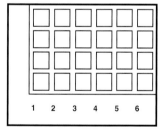

PREPARING AND CUTTING CANVAS
Before cutting out your pieces, notice the thread count of each piece on your chart. The thread count is usually located above the piece on the chart. The thread count tells you the number of threads in the width and the height of the canvas piece. Follow the thread count to cut out a rectangle the specified size. Remember to count **threads**, not **holes**. If you accidentally count holes, your piece is going to be the wrong size. Follow the chart to trim the rectangle into the desired shape.

You may want to mark the outline of the piece on your canvas before cutting it out. Use a China marker or a grease pencil to draw the outline of your shape on the canvas. Before you begin stitching, be sure to remove all markings with a dry tissue or paper towel. Any remaining markings are likely to rub off on your yarn as you stitch.

A good pair of household scissors is recommended for cutting plastic canvas. However, a craft knife is helpful when cutting a small area from the center of a larger piece of canvas. For example, a craft knife is recommended for cutting the opening out of a tissue box cover top. When using a craft knife, be sure to protect the table below your canvas. A layer of cardboard or a magazine should provide enough padding to protect your table.

When cutting canvas, be sure to cut as close to the thread as possible without cutting into the thread. If you don't cut close enough, "nubs" or "pickets" will be left on the edge of your canvas. Be sure to cut off all nubs from the canvas before you begin to stitch, because nubs will snag the yarn and are difficult to cover.

When cutting plastic canvas along a diagonal, cut through the center of each intersection. This will leave enough plastic canvas on both sides of the cut so that both pieces of canvas may be used. Diagonal corners will also snag yarn less and be easier to cover.

The charts may show slits in the plastic canvas (Fig. 2). To make slits, use a craft knife to cut exactly through the center of an intersection of plastic canvas threads (Fig. 3). Repeat for number of intersections needed. When working piece, be careful not to carry yarn across slits.

Fig. 2

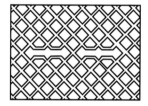

Fig. 3

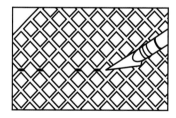

If your project has several pieces, you may want to cut them all out before you begin stitching. Keep your cut pieces in a sealable plastic bag to prevent loss.

THREADING YOUR NEEDLE

Many people wonder, "What is the best way to thread my needle?" Here are a couple of methods. Practice each one with a scrap of yarn and see what works best for you. There are also several yarn-size needle threaders available at your local craft store.

FOLD METHOD

First, sharply fold the end of yarn over your needle; then remove needle. Keeping the fold sharp, push the needle onto the yarn (Fig. 4).

Fig. 4

THREAD METHOD

Fold a 5" piece of sewing thread in half, forming a loop. Insert loop of thread through the eye of your needle (Fig. 5). Insert yarn through the loop and pull the thread back through your needle, pulling yarn through at the same time.

Fig. 5

WASHING INSTRUCTIONS

If you used washable yarn for all of your stitches, you may hand wash plastic canvas projects in warm water with a mild soap. Do not rub or scrub stitches; this will cause the yarn to fuzz. Allow your stitched piece to air dry. Do not put stitched pieces in a clothes dryer. The plastic canvas could melt in the heat of a dryer. Do not dry clean your plastic canvas. The chemicals used in dry cleaning could dissolve the plastic canvas. When piece is dry, you may need to trim the fuzz from your project with a small pair of sharp scissors.

GENERAL INFORMATION

1. **Fig. 1**, page 45, shows how to count threads accurately. Follow charts to cut out plastic canvas pieces.
2. Backstitch used for detail (**Fig. 7**) and French Knots (**Fig. 10**) are worked over completed stitches.
3. Unless otherwise indicated, Overcast Stitches (**Fig. 12**) are used to cover edges of pieces and to join pieces.

STITCH DIAGRAMS

> Unless otherwise indicated, bring threaded needle up at 1 and all odd numbers and down at 2 and all even numbers.

ALTERNATING SCOTCH STITCH

This Scotch Stitch variation is worked over three or more threads, forming alternating blocks (Fig. 6).

Fig. 6

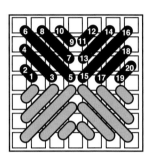

BACKSTITCH

This stitch is worked over completed stitches to outline or define (Fig. 7). It is sometimes worked over more than one thread. Backstitch may also be used to cover canvas as shown in Fig. 8.

Fig. 7

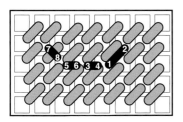

Fig. 8

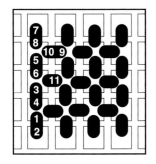

CROSS STITCH

This stitch is composed of two stitches (Fig. 9). The top stitch of each cross must always be made in the same direction. The number of intersections may vary according to the chart.

Fig. 9

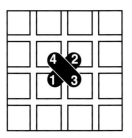

FRENCH KNOT

Bring needle up through hole. Wrap yarn once around needle and insert needle in same hole or adjacent hole, holding end of yarn with non-stitching fingers (Fig. 10). Tighten knot; then pull needle through canvas, holding yarn until it must be released.

Fig. 10

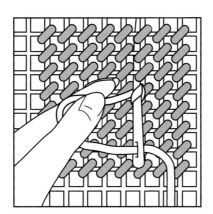

GOBELIN STITCH

This basic straight stitch is worked over two or more threads or intersections. The number of threads or intersections may vary according to the chart (Fig. 11).

Fig. 11

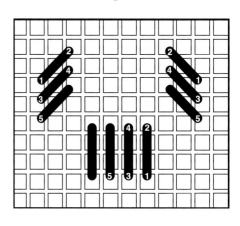

OVERCAST STITCH

This stitch covers the edge of the canvas and joins pieces of canvas (Fig. 12). It may be necessary to go through the same hole more than once to get even coverage on the edge, especially at the corners.

Fig. 12

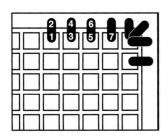

SCOTCH STITCH

These slanted straight stitches are worked over three or more threads as shown in Fig. 13, to form a square.

Fig. 13

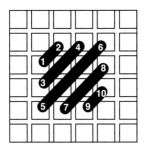

TENT STITCH

This stitch is worked in vertical or horizontal rows over one intersection as shown in Fig. 14. Follow Fig. 15 to work the **Reversed Tent Stitch**.

Fig. 14

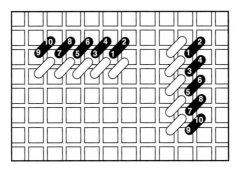

Fig. 15

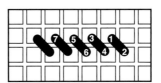

Sometimes when you are working Tent Stitches, the last stitch on the row will look "pulled" on the front of your piece when you are changing directions. To avoid this problem, leave a loop of yarn on the wrong side of the stitched piece after making the last stitch in the row. When making the first stitch in the next row, run your needle through the loop (Fig. 16). Gently pull yarn until all stitches are even.

Fig. 16

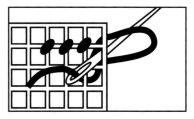

TRIPLE CROSS STITCH

This square stitch is worked over three horizontal and three vertical threads (Fig. 17). Each stitch is worked completely before going on to the next.

Fig. 17

Production Team: Technical Writer - Lisa Lancaster; Technical Associate - Mary Sullivan Hutcheson; Editorial Writer - Susan Frantz Wiles; Senior Graphic Artist - Lora Puls; and Graphic Artist - Victoria Temple.